GW01458346

He

Se

Advisory

Committee

. . . .

Anaesthetic agents: Controlling exposure under COSHH

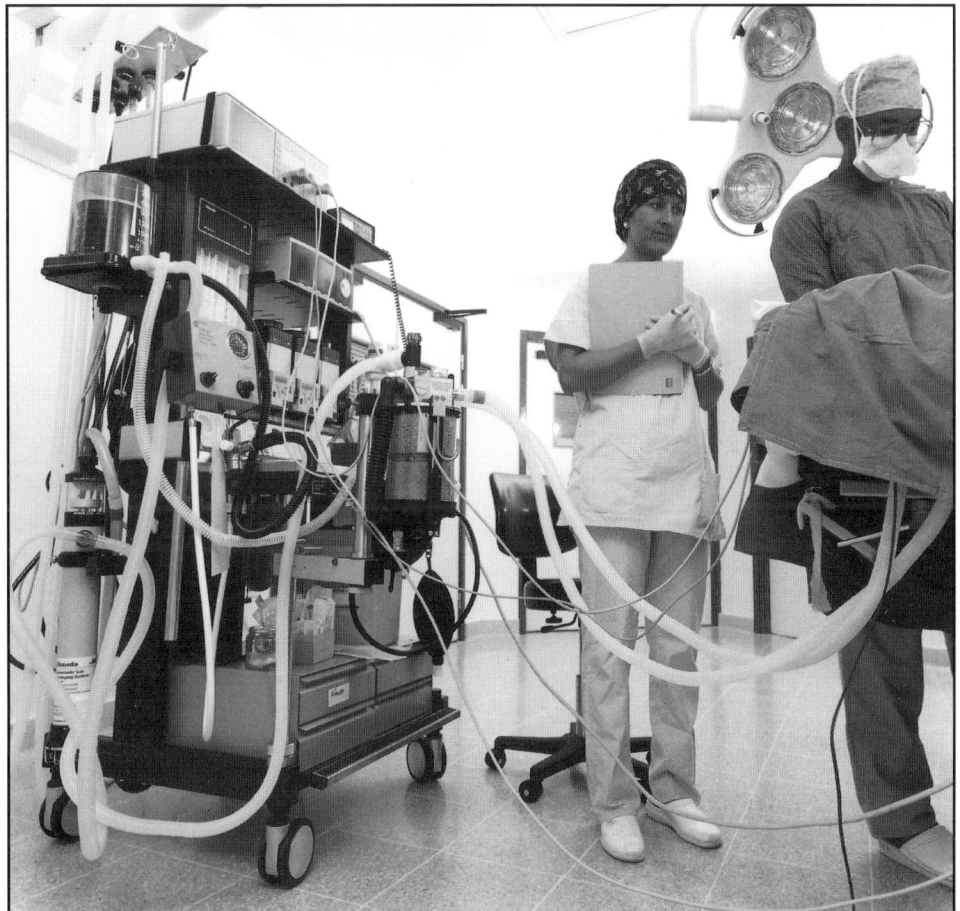

HSE BOOKS

© Crown copyright 1995

Applications for reproduction should be made to HMSO

First published 1995

ISBN 0 7176 1043 8

This is guidance prepared, in consultation with HSE and the Department of Health, by the Health Services Advisory Committee which was appointed by the Health and Safety Commission as part of its formal advisory structures. The guidance represents what is considered to be good practice by the members of the Committee. It has been agreed by the Commission. Following this guidance is not compulsory and you are free to take other action. But if you do follow this guidance you will normally be doing enough to comply with the law. Health and safety inspectors seek to secure compliance with the law and may refer to this guidance as illustrating good practice.

Photographs by courtesy of
Frenchay Healthcare NHS Trust
Great Ormond Street Hospital for Children
Health and Scientific Construction Ltd

CONTENTS

FOREWORD

This guidance has been prepared by the Health Services Advisory Committee in liaison with the Health and Safety Executive and the Department of Health. It suggests to health services employers, and health care professionals and all those who are involved in health and safety management how to comply with the key parts of the Control of Substances Hazardous to Health (COSHH) Regulations 1994 and with the Occupational Exposure Standards (OESs) for the four anaesthetic agents - nitrous oxide, halothane, enflurane and isoflurane. The OESs will come into force in January 1996. Although the guidance may be applicable to those involved in primary health care, it is primarily aimed at those working in the secondary health care sector.

The guidance explains how the OESs will help to protect the health of your employees, the legal framework in which they operate and gives practical advice on how to comply with the law. It covers the three main areas where anaesthetic agents are used - general anaesthesia - inhalation analgesia - cryocautery. Although we have not specifically considered veterinary practices, much of the guidance will apply to the control of exposure to anaesthetic agents in veterinary surgeries.

INTRODUCTION

1   For a number of years there has been concern among both employees and employers about possible risks to health from repeated exposure to anaesthetic agents. All the available information on toxic effects has been examined by the Health and Safety Commission's Advisory Committee on Toxic Substances (ACTS). This committee concluded that there may be a risk to health from repeated exposure to persistently high levels of anaesthetic agents, but levels could be identified at which there is no significant risk to health. Consequently ACTS recommended that Occupational Exposure Standards (OESs) were necessary to protect the health of those regularly exposed.

2   The OESs for anaesthetic agents, which will come into force upon publication of EH40 early in 1996, are:

   (a) 100 ppm for nitrous oxide over an 8 hour Time Weighted Average reference period;

   (b) 50 ppm for enflurane over an 8 hour Time Weighted Average reference period;

   (c) 50 ppm for isoflurane over an 8 hour Time Weighted Average reference period; and

   (d) 10 ppm for halothane over an 8 hour Time Weighted Average reference period.

EFFECTS OF EXPOSURE TO ANAESTHETIC AGENTS

3   At high concentrations of several thousand parts per million (ppm) all anaesthetic agents, by definition, reduce activity in the nervous system, leading to anaesthesia. In contrast to patients who may be exposed to these high concentrations a few times in their lives, health care staff may be exposed day after day to much lower concentrations. There have been a number of reports in scientific literature claiming that such exposures can lead to adverse health effects, particularly an increased risk of miscarriage. However, other studies have not found these effects. Paragraphs 4 to 9 summarise the evidence for adverse health effects and explain the reasoning behind the OES values set by the HSC.

Nitrous oxide   4   There have been many studies of health care workers to investigate whether or not nitrous oxide produces adverse effects on the developing embryo or fetus. There are many uncertainties in studies of this type and in none were there any reliable estimates of the amount of nitrous oxide inhaled by the study group. Some studies claimed positive results, others appeared negative and some criticisms can be levelled at the reliability and robustness of the studies. Overall, there is no convincing human evidence that exposure to nitrous oxide in the workplace has caused developmental defects in the fetus or any other reproductive health effects.

5   The evidence for adverse effects has also been considered in animals. Studies in which rats were repeatedly or continuously exposed to high exposures (1000 ppm and above for eight hours or more a day) of nitrous oxide showed evidence of developmental toxicity to the embryo/fetus. No effects were seen in animals similarly exposed to 500 ppm. Laboratory studies suggest that this effect occurs because nitrous oxide can inhibit the production of new cells. Since this could also occur in humans, the potential for nitrous oxide to cause developmental effects and other consequences of inhibiting the production of new cells in humans at high exposures cannot be dismissed. An Occupational Exposure Standard has been set at 100 ppm over an 8 hour Time Weighted Average (TWA) reference period. This is a fifth of the exposure level at which **no effects** were seen in experimental animal studies and represents a level at which there is no evidence to suggest that human health would be affected.

The volatile agents - halothane, isoflurane and enflurane

6   Similarly for the volatile agents, from the studies of health care workers there is no convincing evidence that they have caused adverse reproductive effects.

7   However, there is evidence from animal studies that both halothane and isoflurane can induce adverse effects on the development of the fetus during pregnancy. Yet these effects have been seen following repeated exposures at 1000 ppm and above. There is no convincing evidence for any other adverse effects in animals from repeated exposure up to at least 100 ppm for halothane and 600 ppm for isoflurane.

8   There is no evidence from animal studies to indicate that enflurane has any adverse effect on the developing fetus. Compared to the other anaesthetic agents enflurane is noticeably less toxic, though liver damage was seen in mice following continuous exposures of 700 ppm and above.

9   Therefore the values chosen for the OESs for the volatile agents are well below the levels at which any significant adverse effects occurred in animals and represent levels at which there is no evidence to suggest human health would be affected.

THE CONTROL OF SUBSTANCES HAZARDOUS TO HEALTH REGULATIONS 1994 (COSHH)

10   The Control of Substances Hazardous to Health Regulations 1994 (COSHH) set out the legal requirements for protecting the health of people in the workplace from hazardous substances: anaesthetic gases and volatile agents are covered by COSHH. The requirements of COSHH do not apply to a patient to whom anaesthetic gases and volatile agents are administered in the course of medical treatment. The Regulations apply to people who are exposed to anaesthetic gases and volatile agents during the course of their work. This guidance sets out the main provisions of the COSHH Regulations in relation to the OESs and gives advice on how to comply with them. For more general information on COSHH, see the reference section on page 17.

OCCUPATIONAL EXPOSURE STANDARDS

11   COSHH requires employers to ensure that the exposure of their employees to substances hazardous to health is either prevented, or where this is not reasonably practicable, adequately controlled. For a substance which has been assigned an OES, exposure by inhalation should be reduced to that standard.

SAFETY REPRESENTATIVES

12   Where trade union safety representatives are appointed under the Safety Representatives and Safety Committees Regulations 1977, as amended by the Management of Health and Safety at Work Regulations 1992, they must be consulted by the employer. Such consultations allow the safety representatives to assist employers in developing control measures.

ADVICE ON COMPLYING WITH KEY ASPECTS OF THE COSHH REGULATIONS

Assessing the risks to health

Regulation 6 (in part)

(1)   An employer shall not carry out any work which is liable to expose any employees to any substance hazardous to health unless he has made a suitable and sufficient assessment of the risks created by that work to the health of those employees and of the steps that need to be taken to meet the requirements of these Regulations.

Action checklist

- **Where is exposure likely to occur?**

- **Who is likely to be exposed?**

- **Estimate exposure.**

- **Compare exposure to the OESs.**

- **If exposures exceed or are likely to exceed the OESs, decide what control measures you need.**

- **Review assessment regularly.**

---

13   You will need to carry out a 'suitable and sufficient' risk assessment where exposure to anaesthetic gases and volatile agents is likely to occur.

14   In the first instance you will need to estimate the level of exposure, taking into account the scavenging and ventilation equipment and systems of work currently employed for controlling exposure. You should then compare the estimate with the OESs. If you can demonstrate that your estimate of exposure is unlikely to exceed the OESs, you do not need to take any further action.

How to estimate exposure

Operating theatres

15   COSHH requires precautions to be taken for the protection of every employee who may be exposed to hazardous substances. In the case of anaesthetic gases and volatile agents, experience shows that in the operating theatre the anaesthetist will generally encounter the highest exposures. It will therefore normally only be necessary to estimate his or her exposure to determine adequate protection for all staff present during operations.

Action checklist

In order to estimate exposure in the operating theatre, you will need to consider the following:

- **For what period of time are the staff exposed?**

- **Is there a gas scavenging system in place?**

- **How effective is the ventilation?**

- **Is there any leakage from the anaesthetic equipment and breathing circuit and the scavenging system into the operating theatre?**

- **Is the gas flow turned off when not in use?**

- **Are vaporisers filled in ventilated areas or filled and drained with 'keyed filling devices'?**

---

16   If you are using active gas scavenging to the British Standard BS 6834:1994 and your ventilation complies with the recommendations in Health Technical Memorandum (HTM) 2025 and Health Building Note (HBN) 26 and there is no significant leakage from the anaesthetic system, it is unlikely that you will exceed the OESs.

Inhalation analgesia in obstetrics and dentistry

Action checklist

In order to estimate exposure in obstetrics and dentistry you will need to consider the following:

- For what period of time are staff exposed?

- How well is the room ventilated?

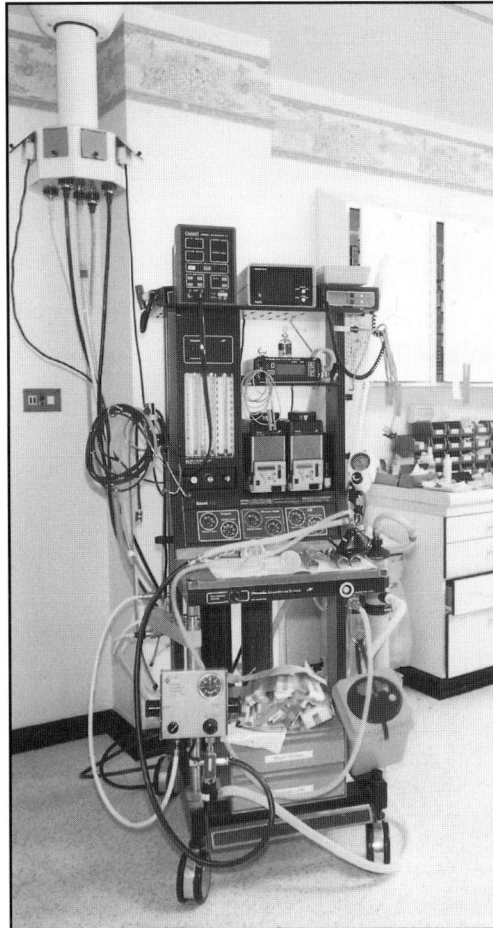

Typical anaesthetic machine with active gas scavenging system to British Standard 6834:1994

17   When nitrous oxide is used as an analgesic, staff could be exposed to high concentrations, but if this is only for short periods their exposures are unlikely to exceed the OES.

Recovery rooms

Action checklist

In order to estimate exposure in recovery rooms you will need to consider the following:

- For what period of time are staff exposed?

- How well is the room ventilated?

Measuring exposures

Remember COSHH applies to personal exposures averaged over 8 hours (an 8 hour TWA).

18   If you cannot easily estimate exposure levels you may need to carry out some personal sampling as part of your risk assessment. (See page 9 for more information).

19   If this is necessary you will **not** normally need to measure each anaesthetic agent separately. Where the volatile agents are being used in conjunction with nitrous oxide you will only need to measure exposure to nitrous oxide, as adequate control of this gas generally implies adequate control of other inhalation anaesthetic agents. (See page 9 for more information on measuring exposure.)

20   If you use the volatile agents extensively and independently of nitrous oxide, you will have to carry out a separate risk assessment. However, in most cases this will not be necessary.

Remember you will need to regularly review your assessment, particularly if you significantly change equipment or procedure.

21   COSHH does not prescribe how often you should review your assessment. We advise that you normally consider reviewing your assessment at least every five years. However, you will need to review it right away if there are significant changes to your equipment and/or working practices.

22   You do not necessarily need to keep a written record of the assessment, but it would be good practice to do so. In the simplest and most obvious cases which can be easily repeated and explained at any time you do not need to keep a written record. However, in most cases it will need to be recorded, particularly if any exposure measurements are taken. A written record is a useful way to demonstrate compliance with the Regulations and will help to ensure that you properly review the assessment when necessary.

Prevention or control of exposure
Regulation 7 (in part)

(1)   *Every employer shall ensure that the exposure of his employees to substances hazardous to health is either prevented or where this is not reasonably practicable, adequately controlled.*

> **Action checklist**
>
> •   **Do exposures exceed the OESs?**
>
> •   **If they do, decide what control measures you need.**
>
> •   **Implement necessary control measures.**

23   As it is not generally possible to completely prevent exposure to anaesthetic agents, exposure must be adequately controlled. Adequate control is demonstrated by keeping exposure in line with the OESs. So to comply with COSHH and the OESs for anaesthetic agents you will have to make sure that personal exposure to anaesthetic agents over a TWA of eight hours is reduced to:

(a) 100 ppm for nitrous oxide;

(b) 50 ppm for enflurane;

(c) 50 ppm for isoflurane; and

(d) 10 ppm for halothane.

24 This means that exposure to anaesthetic agents is adequately controlled if the average exposure is reduced to the OES over an eight hour period. Short term excursions above the standard do not infringe COSHH provided the average exposure over eight hours does not exceed the standard.

25   If your risk assessment reveals that exposure is likely to exceed the OESs you should find out why and take appropriate steps to comply with the OESs as soon as is reasonably practicable. You will not be in breach of the law if you take this action. When deciding what is a "reasonably practicable" timescale for compliance, you will need to balance the extent of exposure against the cost of control measures.

26   To achieve adequate control you may need to consider adopting some or even all of the control measures laid out under the section headed 'Recommended control measures' on page 11.

Use of control measures

Regulation 8 (in part)

Every employer who provides any control measure, personal protective equipment or other thing or facility pursuant to these Regulations shall take all reasonable steps to ensure that it is properly used or applied as the case may be.

Action checklist

- **Make sure employees use control measures correctly.** ✔

- **Make sure that your employees are properly trained to use the control measures you provide.**

- **Make clear to employees the importance of reporting any defects in engineering controls.**

Maintenance, examination and testing of control measures

Regulation 9 (in part)

(1) Every employer who provides any control measure to meet the requirements of Regulation 7 shall ensure that it is maintained in an efficient state, in efficient working order and in good repair.

Action checklist   ✔

- **Check your equipment for controlling exposure is in good working order.**

- **Have your scavenging and ventilation equipment regularly serviced.**

---

27 You should:

(a) examine and test control measures at suitable or specified intervals;

(b) visually check at least once a week that scavenging and ventilation equipment is working properly;

(c) have scavenging equipment and ventilation systems regularly serviced in accordance with the manufacturer's recommendations and at least every 14 months; and

(d) periodically review how you operate scavenging equipment to make sure that it is being used correctly.

Monitoring exposure at the workplace

Regulation 10 (in part)

(1) In any case in which -

(a) it is requisite for ensuring the maintenance of adequate control of the exposure of employees to substances hazardous to health ... the employer shall ensure that the exposure of employees to substances hazardous to health is monitored in accordance with a suitable procedure.

Action checklist   ✔

A programme of routine monitoring of exposure will not normally be necessary. You will only need to consider monitoring if:

- **you think control measures may be inadequate;**

- **you change your working practices; or**

- **your COSHH assessment shows wide variations in exposure.**

---

28   The result of your COSHH assessment will tell you whether you need to introduce a programme of monitoring. If your COSHH assessment shows that you are unlikely to exceed the OESs you will not normally need to follow a monitoring programme. However, monitoring may be necessary when:

(a)   you change procedure and/or equipment which may significantly affect anaesthetic gas and volatile agent control (but this will probably mean that you should carry out a reassessment. See page 3);

(b)   your COSHH assessment reveals that there are, or may be, wide variations of exposure at certain times and in certain places, eg in areas such as paediatric surgery and dentistry where scavenging or other control measures may not be reasonably practicable and there may be potential for higher exposures. This might lead you to consider controlling the duration of exposure.

How to sample   29   If you do find that it is necessary to monitor exposure or to measure exposure as part of your COSHH assessment, you will need to determine personal exposure levels by taking time weighted air samples in the breathing zone of those potentially most exposed. Personal diffusive sampling techniques are suitable for measuring exposure to anaesthetic agents and are the most cost effective method available. Diffusive samplers are small and easily attached to clothing.

30   You will normally need to sample nitrous oxide only, as adequate control of this gas implies adequate control of other inhalational anaesthetic agents. You will only need separate sampling for the volatile agents if they are used independently of nitrous oxide on a regular basis.

31   You can keep sampling to a minimum if:

(a)   you sample worst case situations only - this will help you identify real priorities;

(b)   you only sample areas where staff are regularly exposed to anaesthetic agents - it is not necessary to sample in a room used occasionally for emergencies;

(c)   you sample only those staff likely to receive the highest exposures, ie:

(i)   in the operating theatre sampling the breathing zone of the anaesthetist will generally give you a clear indication of whether or not you are complying with the OESs;

(ii)   in midwifery sampling one midwife who is substantially exposed to nitrous oxide/oxygen mixtures will again generally give you a clear indication of whether you are complying with the OES.

32   To monitor nitrous oxide you can use a diffusive sampler filled with molecular sieve-5A. Further details are given in reference A (see page 16).

33   If you decide you need to measure exposure to the volatile agents you will need a separate sampling tube. However, you can use this tube for all the volatile agents. The details of the most cost effective sampling method can be found in reference B (see page 16).

Health surveillance

Regulation 11 (in part)

    (1) Where it is appropriate for the protection of the health of his employees who are, or are liable to be, exposed to a substance hazardous to health, the employer shall ensure that such employees are under suitable health surveillance.

Health surveillance is not necessary for normal use of anaesthetic agents.

Informing and training employees

Regulation 12 (in part)

    (1) An employer who undertakes work which may expose any of his employees to substances hazardous to health shall provide that employee with such information, instruction and training as is suitable and sufficient to know -

    (a) the risks to health created by such exposure; and

    (b) the precautions which should be taken.

Action checklist

- **Make sure your employees know the possible risks to their health of exposure to anaesthetic gases and volatile agents.**

- **Make sure your employees understand the need for control measures.**

- **Make sure your employees understand how to use the control measures.**

- **Provide information to employees on the results of any monitoring you may have carried out.**

---

34   You will need to make sure that your employees:

    (a) are aware that there may be risks to health from exposure to anaesthetic agents. You may wish to discuss this booklet with them;

(b) know why control measures such as scavenging and ventilation are necessary and how to use them properly;

(c) know the arrangements you have made for providing information on the results of any monitoring you may carry out. You will also need to make this information available to employees' representatives.

RECOMMENDED CONTROL MEASURES

General anaesthesia

Action checklist

To adequately control exposure to anaesthetic agents in the operating theatre you will probably need to:

- **use a scavenging system to remove pollution at source;**

- **ventilate the room to infection control standards to dilute pollution from leaks;**

- **follow good housekeeping to minimise leakage from poorly fitted face masks, flow meters inadvertently left on, poorly maintained anaesthetic or scavenging equipment.**

---

35 There are several different types of breathing circuit used to administer anaesthetic agents to the patient, depending on the procedure to be carried out. For general anaesthesia, nearly all breathing systems incorporate either an expiratory valve or a port on the ventilator to which you can connect a scavenging system. Make sure that these comply with British Standard BS 6834:1994. The exceptions are paediatric breathing circuits where you may not be able to connect a scavenging system directly. Guidance on scavenging systems is given in HTM 2022 *Medical gas pipeline systems.*

36 The main sources of pollution are:

(a) excess gas from the expiratory valve on the breathing system;

(b) discharge from the expiratory port of the ventilator;

(c) expired air from the patient;

(d) leakage from equipment, poorly fitting face mask;

(e) spillage from the receiving system of the active gas scavenging (AGS) system;

(f) discharge from gas monitoring equipment.

37 To minimise pollution from leaks, check there are no significant leaks in the breathing hoses, the breathing bag, or from poor connectors, and from around the face mask.

38 To minimise the pollution from spillage from the receiving system of the AGS system, check you are using an appropriate scavenging system, the disposal system is not blocked and the extract system is working. Make sure that the filter is clean and that the flow indicator is working.

39 If you use a closed circuit system for administering anaesthesia and monitor the breathing gases using an analyser, check that the sample collected is piped into the AGS system and not into the ambient air.

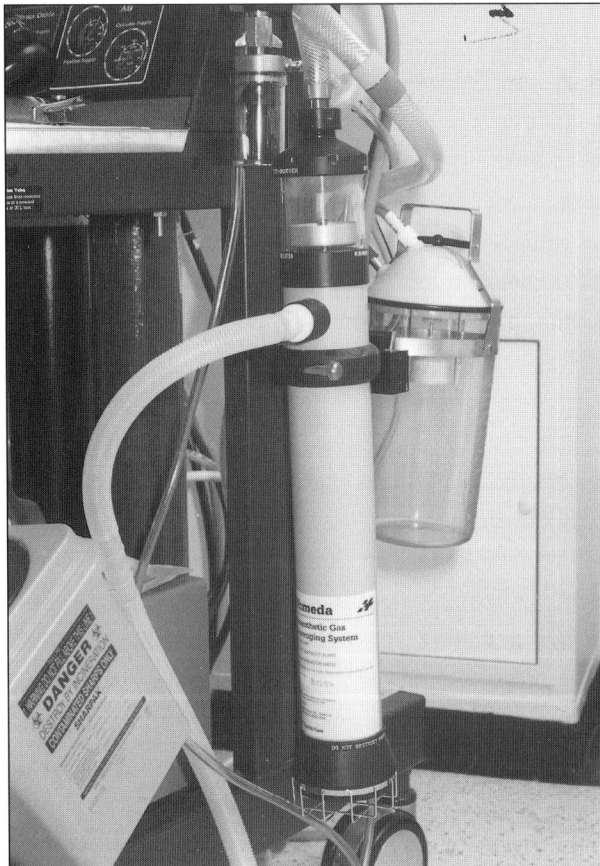

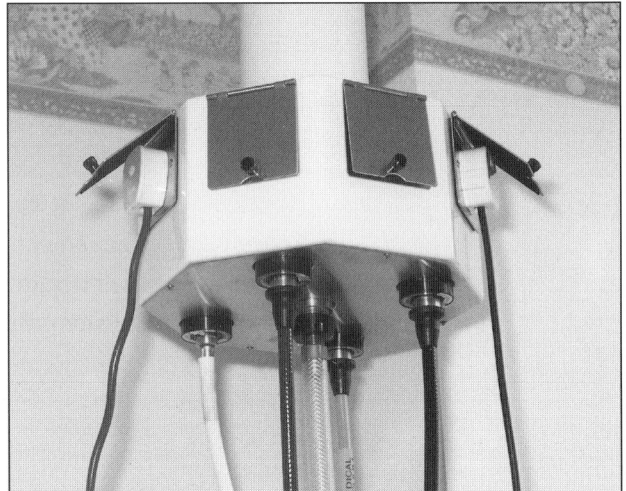

Above: Ceiling pendant with active gas scavenging system terminal unit

Left: The receiving system

Gas scavenging equipment

40 AGS systems can only remove pollution captured at source. This means that you should preferably use an AGS system to remove pollution from anaesthetic breathing systems incorporating an expiratory valve or port which complies with the requirements of BS 6834:1994.

41 You will normally need AGS terminal units in areas where you routinely administer general anaesthetics - anaesthetic rooms and operating theatres - to control exposure to the OESs.

42 Your COSHH assessment will tell you whether you need to provide AGS systems in areas where you use anaesthetic agents less frequently, eg X-ray and endoscopy departments.

43 If your AGS system complies with British Standard BS 6834:1994, it is unlikely that you will exceed the OESs, particularly if the ventilation in the theatre complies with HTM 2025 and HBN 26.

44 You may already have scavenging equipment which does not conform to the British Standard. This may still control exposure to the OESs. Your COSHH assessment will tell you whether or not you need to take further action. However, bear in mind that passive and semi-passive scavenging systems may not control exposure to the OESs. You may need to monitor exposure to check their performance.

Ventilation

45 The ventilation of operating theatres to control infection and the environment also helps to control exposure to anaesthetic agents. HBN 26 gives information on recommended ventilation standards for aerobiological and environmental control and the design considerations part of HTM 2025: *Ventilation in health care premises* gives guidance on ventilation systems. It recommends that the air movement should ensure that any leakage of anaesthetic agents is diluted and removed from the theatre suite. This particularly applies to short procedures as the ventilation system dilutes the pollution between cases.

Paediatric anaesthesia

46 The Jackson-Rees modification of the Ayres T- piece (Mapleson E circuit) open ended reservoir bag is often used in paediatric anaesthesia. You may not always be able to use an AGS system with these types of paediatric breathing systems. A specially designed scavenging valve is available for use with these circuits but it is not appropriate for all applications.

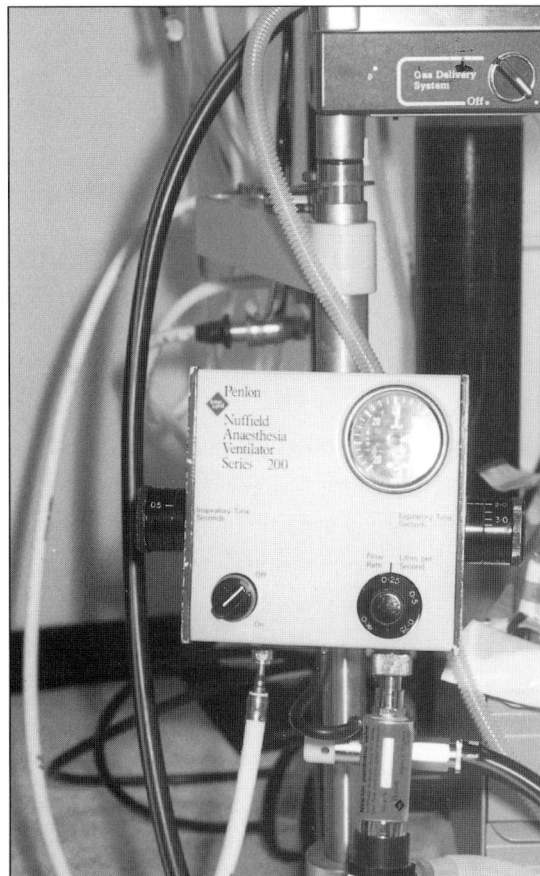

47 It is possible to use an AGS system if the patient is ventilated, since the AGS system can be connected to the expiratory port of the ventilator. For paediatric applications, care should be taken to ensure that excessive positive or negative pressure is not applied to the patient circuit. An appropriate valve such as the Newton paediatric valve together with a safety block should be used in accordance with the manufacturer's instructions.

Nuffield ventilator with Newton paediatric scavenging valve

48 In many cases in paediatric anaesthesia, including induction, it will not be possible to use an AGS system to remove the polluted gas at source. Therefore the room ventilation will need to be adequate to dilute and remove the pollution. Ventilation systems which comply with HTM 2025 generally control exposure to the OESs.

Inhalation analgesia in obstetrics and dentistry

49 Inhalation analgesia is used for pain relief and reduction of anxiety in patients during childbirth, dentistry and occasionally physiotherapy, ITU and acute wards using a nitrous oxide/oxygen mixture. The main source of pollution is the patient's exhaled breath and leaks from the breathing circuit and face masks. It is not normally possible to use an AGS system when nitrous oxide is administered as an analgesic.

Dentistry

50 It is unlikely that staff in a dental surgery will be exposed to levels in excess of the OES if, as is often the case, anaesthetic gas is used for only one or two sessions a week. If you find you are exceeding the OES you will need to improve the ventilation. You can find guidance on ventilation requirements in HBN 12 *Out patients department, Supplement 2*. These requirements are primarily for patient comfort, but they will also help to control exposure to nitrous oxide.

51 Dental procedures involving general anaesthesia are covered by the section on general anaesthesia (see page 11).

Obstetrics

52 In obstetrics you will have to rely on the room ventilation and good housekeeping techniques to control exposure, including making sure there are no significant leaks from the equipment.

53 HBN 21 *Maternity department* recommends that balanced supply and extract ventilation is provided within the range of 6-7 air changes per hour for delivery rooms. This is mainly for patient comfort, but it will also help to control exposure to nitrous oxide.

54 However, your COSHH assessment may show that you are complying with the OES with fewer air changes. Oxygen/nitrous oxide mixtures are used intermittently from several minutes up to several hours. Generally, however, staff are only exposed for part of their working day, and it is therefore unlikely that their exposures will exceed the OES, although the short term exposures can be high.

55 Obstetric procedures involving general anaesthesia are covered by the section on general anaesthesia (see page 11).

Recovery areas

56 In recovery areas, the major source of pollution is from the patient's exhaled breath. You will need to rely on general ventilation to control exposure. You can find guidance on the design of ventilation systems for recovery areas in HTM 2025. It recommends 15 air changes per hour are provided with a balanced flow. Where possible, the supply air terminal should be ceiling mounted above the recovery bed positions so that anaesthetic agents breathed out by recovering patients will be diluted immediately. However, you may already be complying with the OESs with fewer air changes. Your COSHH assessment will tell you whether you need to improve the ventilation.

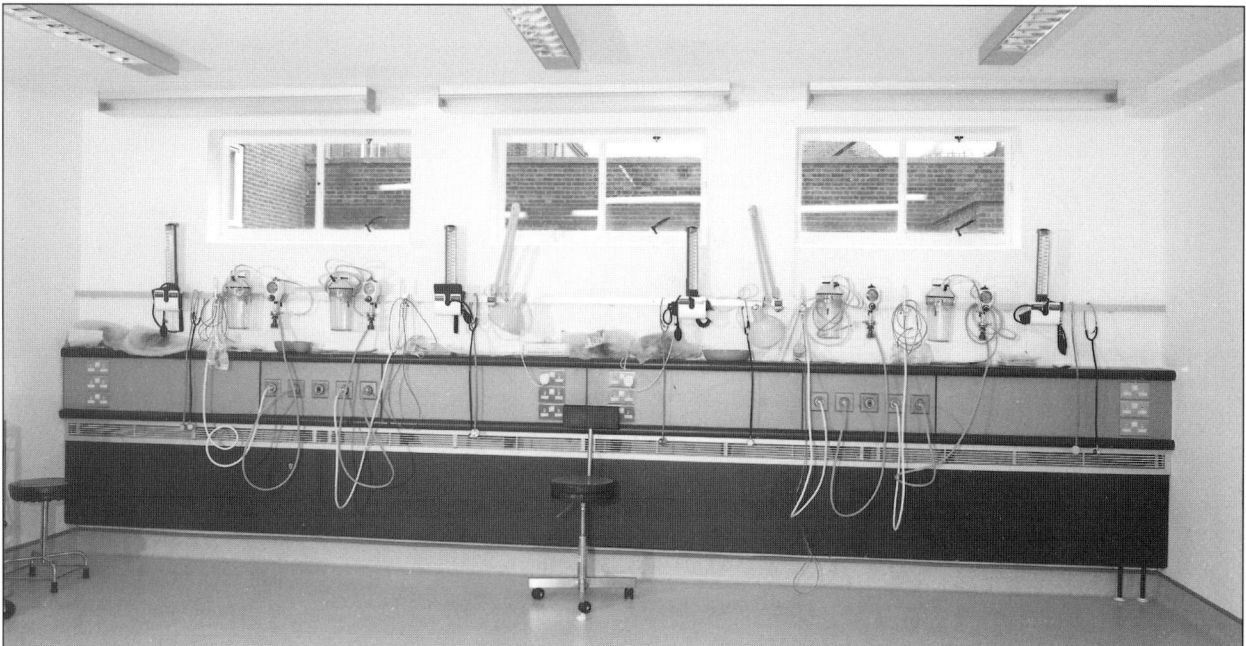

Recovery area with extract ventilation

Ambulances

57 Nitrous oxide and oxygen mixtures are also used for pain relief of patients in ambulance vehicles. As the patient's use of the gas generally varies from a few minutes to 15 minutes at a time, adequate ventilation is usually provided from open windows and/or roof vents. Your COSHH assessment will tell you whether or not you need to improve your ventilation.

Cryocautery probes

58 If you use nitrous oxide to cool cryocautery probes you can collect the gas from the probes and take it via a tube to a safe discharge point. The discharge tube can be taken to an extract terminal of a non-recirculating exhaust ventilation system or can be piped to a safe place outside the building. If you do this it is unlikely that you will exceed the OES.

. . . .

REFERENCES

A   *A personal sampling method for the determination of nitrous oxide exposure*
P C Cox and R H Brown, American Industrial Hygiene Association Journal
May 1984 Vol 45 no 5, 345-350

B   *General method for sampling gases and vapours* MDHS 70 HSE Books
ISBN 0 7176 0608 2

Department of Health publications

Health Building Notes   12   *Out patients department*
Sp2 oral surgery, orthodontics, restorative dentistry
Price £30.00 HMSO
ISBN 0 11 321405 7

     21   *Maternity department*
Price £8.00 HMSO
ISBN 0 11 321199 6

     26   *Operating department*
Price £25.00 HMSO
ISBN 0 11 321385 9

Health Technical Memoranda   2022   ***Medical gas pipeline systems***

Management policy
Price £35.00 HMSO
ISBN 0 11 321748 X

Design considerations
Price £50.00 HMSO
ISBN 0 11 321741 1

Validation and verification
Price £50.00 HMSO
ISBN 0 11 321750 1

Operational management
Price £30.00 HMSO
ISBN 0 11 321749 8

Good practice guide
Price £25.00 HMSO
ISBN 0 11 321751 X

2025   **Ventilation in health care premises**

Management policy
Price £35.00 HMSO
ISBN 0 11 321743 9

Design considerations
Price £75.00
ISBN 0 11 321752 8

Validation and verification
Price £25.00 HMSO
ISBN 0 11 321741 2

Operational management
Price £50.00 HMSO
ISBN 0 11 321741 2

Further information
on COSHH

HSC *General COSHH ACOP, Biological agents ACOP* Control of
Substances Hazardous to Health Regulations 1994 Approved Codes
of Practice HSE Books
ISBN 0 7176 0819 0

· ·

Page 18 Health Services Advisory Committee

Printed and published by the Health and Safety Executive   C30   1/96